Dowser's Apprentice

Dowser's Apprentice
Copyright © 2014 Helen Wickes
Paperback ISBN: 978-0-9840352-8-1

All rights reserved: except for the purpose of quoting brief passages for review, no part of this book may be reproduced or transmitted in any form or by any means, electronic or mechanical, including photocopying, recording, or by any information storage and retrieval system, without permission in writing from the publisher.

Cover art: Michael Wickes
Cover design: Steven Asmussen
Design & Layout: Steven Asmussen

Glass Lyre Press, LLC.
P.O. Box 2693
Glenview, IL 60026

www.GlassLyrePress.com

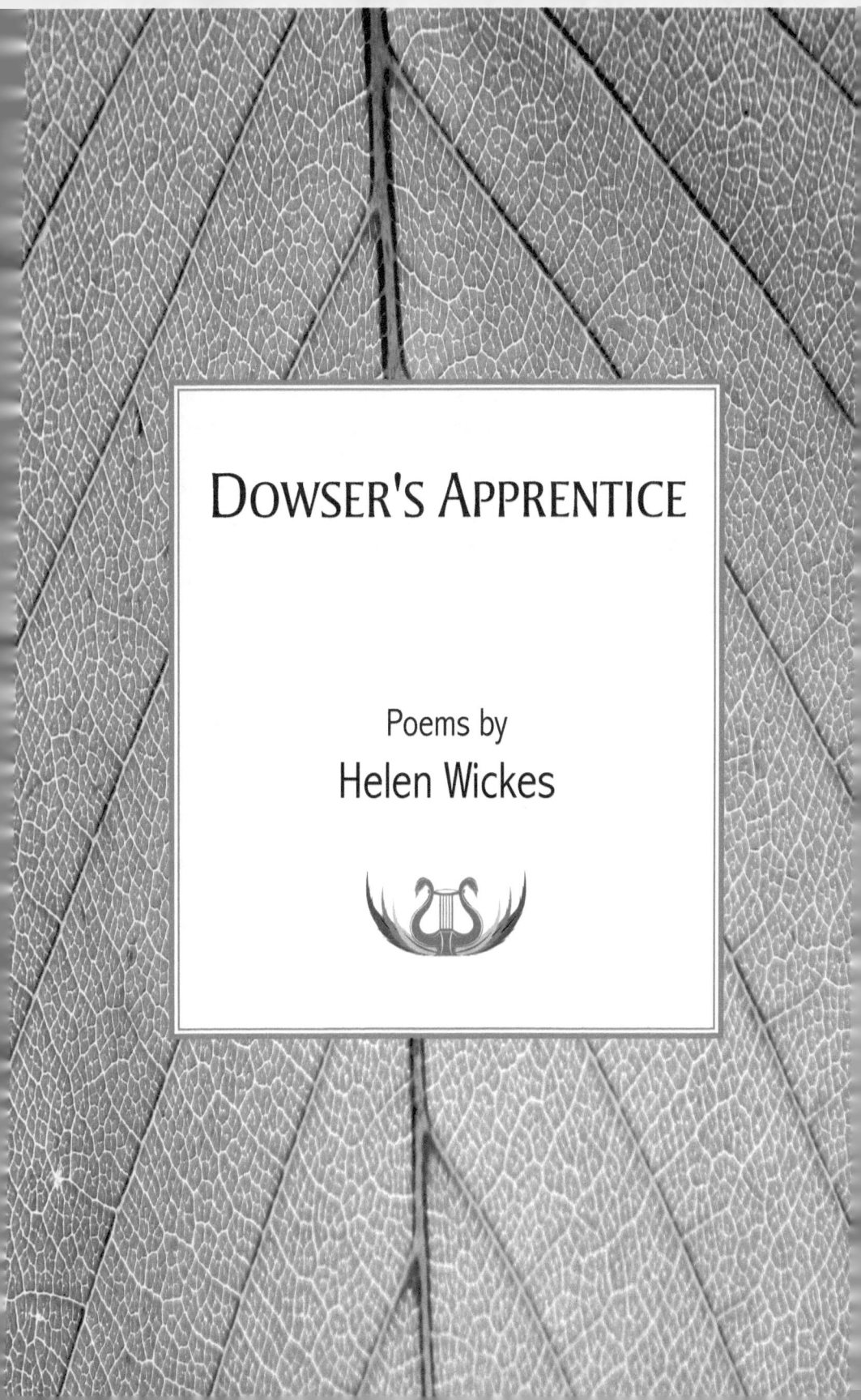

Dowser's Apprentice

Poems by
Helen Wickes

For Don

Thanks to the poets of Sixteen Rivers Press; Murray Silverstein, Gillian Wegener, Lynne Knight, Jerry Fleming, Carolyn Miller; the Whitmaniacs' writing group & David St. John; Richard Silberg & Joyce Jenkins of Poetry Flash, Edward Smallfield, Mark Doty, Amy Gerstler, Ed Ochester, Eve Pell, Jane Hirshfield, Babette Jenny, Marguerite Cunningham, Pina Piccolo, my brothers, Michael and Timothy Wickes; and Don Stang

Acknowledgements

AGNI Online: "Dowser's Apprentice"

Arroyo Literary Review: "Hummingbird"

California Quarterly: "Mushrooms," "Grateful," "New Moon," "Sprouting Moon," "Flower Moon," "The Everyday Dog"

CALYX Journal: "Amputation"

The Citron Review: "Harrow," "Still Life on the Way to Los Ojos," and "The Vagrant Spirit as the Good Humor Man"

Crack the Spine: "Shame," and "Reminders to My Biographer"

Dos Passos Review: "Still Life with Sand in a Picture Locket"

failbetter.com: "The Year my Nouns Left Town"

Ginosko: "Still-Life with Sand in a Picture Locket"

Green Hills Literary Lantern: "Summer Heat"

Hanging Loose Press: "Single Thread"

Kaleidoscope: "Amputation"

MARY: A Journal of New Writing: "Neighbor's Magnolia," "Fifty-Minute Hours," "Ode to a Jeffrey Pine"

Midway Journal: "Shame"

PANK Magazine: "Roofers"

Pirene's Fountain: "Strategies in Pink," "Medicine Chest"

Poetry Flash: "Sunday Morning Go to Town"

Poetry Daily: "Single Thread" was the featured poem on December 12, 2011

Sante Fe Review: "Esthetician to the Elite"

West Marin Review: "The Year My Nouns Left Town"

Willow Review: "Roadside"

Zone 3: "Summer Nights"

Contents

Hurry Up and Break into Life

Summer's Drift	17
Still Life on the Road to Los Ojos	18
Buena Vista, El Dorado County	19
Return to Henderson Canyon	21
Borrego Journal, Sunday	22
Drought Year at Indian Head Rock	23
Medicine Chest	24
California Mission Suite	25
Neighbor's Magnolia	26
Roofers	28
Roadside	30
Ode to a Jeffrey Pine	32
Mountain Lake, September	34

A Door in the Wall, an Open Field

Hell to Heaven Any Given Day	39
Hummingbird	40
Sunday Morning Go to Town	42
Flower Moon	43
Sprouting Moon	44
New Moon	45
Shame	46
Ephemeris in South Florida in Winter	47
Snowbound	49
Single Thread	50
The House of Childhood Talks Back	51
Harrow	52
The Everyday Dog	53
Dowser's Apprentice	54

Apple Blossoms Unloosened

Strategies in Pink	59
Still Life with Sand in a Picture Locket	64
Vermeer's Jacket	65
Esthetician to the Elite	66
Fifty-Minute Hours	68
Summer Nights	69
Walking on the Dead at Montségur	71
Streets of Philadelphia	73
Mushrooms	74
Undone	75
Fields	76
Grateful	77

A Desire to Make Something

The Year My Nouns Left Town	81
Return of the Heart	83
What is Implanted in the Body	84
Amputation	85
Syntactic	86
Passage	87
The Vagrant Spirit as the Good Humor Man	88
Meanwhile, There's Still a War	89
Notes on the Solar Storm	90
Ordinary Cosmology	91
The Year's Missing Second	93
Aftermath	94
Reminders to my Biographer	95

HURRY UP AND BREAK INTO LIFE

I

Summer's Drift

On a man's wrist, on a horse's breath,
the dead find purchase and beg
to be taken along to the mountains.

For grace we cultivate an extra layer of dumbness
and always say yes.

Many people stay lucky,
often wanting too little. Not so the fire.
It pounces from one tree's crown to the next.

In childhood the melancholia is incurable—
a constant *let me see you*. Despite beauty
and years of kindness, the fracturing continues.

I should take my soul to the river twice a year
and wash the meanness out.

Poor words, they were never the danger—
Illumination, it's a physical thing.

From way up here, the river, the traffic
are all one sound. Let me watch the fan lift and set down
the hair on your neck. Lavish hair.
Now look—red and yellow with a smattering
of black and white—boy birds accessorize so well.

Imagine not being alive to this, I say,
to this—after 12 years our western tanager returns.
Well, maybe he's not the same tanager.

Still Life on the Road to Los Ojos

First waking's to sound, the dog hoovering flies
off the floor, wheezing from sinus trouble
and from a scorpion bite.

From sleep, swirling toward me, but refusing to cohere
into faces, my lost people come partway back.

Second waking of the morning has the mind
asking its body, *have we met?* Across the road
where Delfín's butchered a steer,

the coyotes approach for leftovers, cringing
and fleeing all night, waiting to get shot at,

which this time, doesn't happen. The back porch
rocking chair, roiled by the wind, sounds like
it's in a hurry, on a secret mission,

and today's gargoyle crouches on my chest, waiting
for me to wake up. *Can't read your face, sir,
pointy chin in your bony little hands,*

as September flips the pages. What to order
for winter warmth. What you want never quite is,
as happened last week,

when Judith's boy snagged his first rainbow, barely legal,
hand-carried it to fry in butter at the Whistle Stop Café.
The head, tail, and insides missing from his plate,

the child grieved all through dinner, through coffee
and cake, until José went through the trash.

The kid's rescued fish head now stored in the freezer,
and he speaks to it when he needs to.

Buena Vista, El Dorado County

The door's flung open by a man hawking harvester parts,
nearly new. A skinny woman spits into the gutter,
someone across the street not liking that,
so she spits again. Then there's the dust—

an engine grinds the dust to a fine quarrel, while the wind
freshens the tips of the cedar trees, and while
a manic crop duster loops the loop

over sun-blanched fields of corn. The porch notes flicker,
breeze-furled as limp hair from a girl's neck:
help is wanted; calves for sale; reward for stolen
chestnut mare; piano lessons.

Feels like I've lived here all my life. Something about heat
and quiet and the woman at the counter saying, *Honey,
come cool yourself with a fresh-bottled iced cappuccino.*

But two suits drive up and get out of a coupe and say
they'll tear this building down and put up
a real town.

This, the only store in town, is made of rock, dragged
by hand, seven miles, by long-gone Chinese hired hands
who hauled the stone from gold-rush country to here.
And here is nothing but hinterland—outback colony,

supplying what big rollers want. If the town demands
commemoration, they say, they'll nail a plaque to an oak.
My father would have offered to injure the suits' tires

or buy them a beer, Aristotle insisting that ire
requires hyperbole. Me, I'll nurse this cool bottle
of soda between my knees and watch
bachelor buttons bluing the heat wave bluer still.

Return to Henderson Canyon

At dawn the stars swallow back their hard glitter

which emerges in birdsong, the ironwood trees
crackling with sound

as the heat of the day drags its shawl through the air,

and the birds go silent in sunlight,
sunlight which tears open the dandelion,

the fragile, doomed world a huge pot,
we constantly fracture and glue together again.

To smell the creosote plant, cup your hands
around a branch of blossoms, breathe into it,
it breathes back at you its sharp and musty scent.

Bees through the heliotrope, a blue surround,

a durable sound, how does anyone ever
stay present for long.

A cactus thorn in my foot, get the tweezers,
pull there, no, dammit, there!

The leathery flap of the crow crosses, recrosses
your body, my body with his shadow, not doomed, are we?

Yellow pollen between the fingertips
feels midway between air and dust

the rooms we thickly people and unpeople,
desires we lug around, lay out, fold up and zip shut.

Borrego Journal, Sunday

He's brazen at dawn, that one coyote,
squatting to mark his spot,
Mine, his pee announces. *Mine.*

Lightly dive-bombed by a crow, he glances,
yellow eye meets yellow eye. The crow feints
and flaps to a smoke tree, busy

with underwing grooming, like a reprimanded cat.
There's a plastic bag impaled on cactus thorns,
and ancient petroglyphs painted on the granite boulder—

a sun, chain links, scratches and doodles.
I wonder if their creator worried,
Will this line do? Will it last?

Maybe she said, Oh my, what a great hue
of red, now what's for lunch, and hey,
come look at how the granite sparkles.

Drought Year at Indian Head Rock

The clouds are dry sponge and my mind's
another dry sponge; squeeze hard as you like,
not a drop from either one.

If all you've written today is babble, remember—
you're bilingual, so go on and translate.
Get to work on translation.

And rescue that plastic bag, or something
living will choke on it. It's called "refuse"
because it refuses to leave on its own.

All day the frantic birds
stab the canvas bags draped over
each bunch of ripening dates.

How the birds swerve and chatter and
they can't get what they know is there.
It sure puts some sapphire in their song.

There's breeze enough to tear the clouds to bits.
The morning offers itself in chewy mouthfuls,
saying, go ahead, have a bite.

Medicine Chest

To Lure the Muse
My mother set saucers of milk and cookies
on the cellar steps for leprechauns, fairies,
the dead, didn't matter who got there first,
they could squabble for the grub as they pleased.

Insomnia Cure
These little pills are guaranteed to close
your eyes or your money back, your life
back too, all the riven hours, the spilled
and the spoiled, dumped out at your feet.

For the Blues
No cure—no matter if they are a them, an it,
or a he; ask them for the next dance, then
the next one, and a ride home with the top down.

Spell Against Rage
Here's a very fine stopwatch and here's a mountain
where you must linger until the granite
has been ground to sediment beneath your feet.

Recipe for Nirvana
A lot of standing around and remembering
morning dew, pillow of stone, green feathers, and how,
if it chooses, heaven will appear any minute now.

California Mission Suite

Death wouldn't stay out of the poem,
he crept in through every breath,
through the arthritic hands of the old man
propping up the olive branches.

Death sauntered into San Juan Bautista
with its six types of lilac into whose spell
we delivered ourselves
while arguing about the six separate sorrows:

the gently trained, the espaliered,
the harshly pollarded, the one that's dwarfed
to fit the pot, one that languishes from lack
of sun, one from never being noticed.

At San Miguel's, death stared from the huge eye
in a yellow triangle painted above the altar,
as if from a Freemason rite, and trailed us
down Highway 101 to Our Lady of Soledad

where the cat slept under that crucified man,
whose delicately nailed-down feet
have become a scratching post,
and here it lurks in San Antonio de Padua's

roped-off garden. Flowering cherry, pear,
and an old well. I wanted to enter the garden,
throw in a penny, and make a prayer, but the priest
said, No, you cannot enter this garden.

It's about our insurance. You might drown.
In the well, he said, and we're not insured.
Neither for suicide nor for clumsiness.
You'd become my dilemma, he said, don't you see?

Neighbor's Magnolia

Hurry up and break
into life, I say, right now
while I'm watching.
January and everything
too slow. You, the one green-budded tree

I climb upstairs to see,
you're relentlessly bare, not changing
a lick. February is when blooms
unzip. Winter for tracking
the incremental. Wherever it leads.

Hours to practice
the art of naming: pink, magenta, rose,
cup-shaped, goblet-sized, goat-eared,
leathery-petaled—getting you wrong
and wronger. The evening wind

like someone sweeping
a concrete floor. You, the tree,
a woman in too-tight shoes, shifting
her weight. You're strange; you have
no scent, harbor no bird, no squirrel.

Pure and aloof
as the beautiful aunt we disliked
but couldn't stop gawking at.
Positive that she withheld
the one secret we needed to live.

That's you, tree.
But come March it's thanks and farewell.
In a pink swirl your petals blow off.
Why can't they fade, wither, spoil,
age, succumb, instead of flying

straight from prime
to ruin? I prefer Camille to Earhart.
Slow down, why don't you,
green-leaved thing,
pulling us fast, faster.

Roofers

Men are ripping off shingles across the street,
layer after blue, scratchy layer,
wrenching nails and flinging everything down.

The woman who lived there smashed her hip,
and, as she was wheeled away, she rolled her eyes
when they told her she'd be home in a week.

She died alone miles from here.
In a new house—do you want to know
who died there or if they were happy?
I never knew.

The men peel tar paper, toss each other
cans of pop, and clamber to the peak, whooping
with what sounds like joy.

They can see the bridge, the city
rising from the morning mist, the shimmer of water,
and are briefly silent.

In the mountains one summer,
we, too, made a new roof, our mouths full of nails,
Nina Simone on the radio; our tool belts clattering,
we swore we'd never leave.

The men sling blue tarps of trash
toward a truck and miss by a long shot.
Junk in the streets, they whoop again.

My neighbor walks his white dog, lets it pee
on the lavender. If he looked up, he'd see me
twirling a pen, spying.

Because of old, wavy window glass,
outside life is watery—the neighbor,
his dog, the workmen swimming,
the houses floating, a dreamed scene.

When we had nailed the final shingle, a deer
ran beneath us and then a coyote. They circled
the house and ran into the woods, the distance

between them unchanging. Watching was intimate
and awful. It was hard to choose: the deer
who devoured our lettuce or the coyote
with his fierce desire.

Roadside

A fine place to launch a boat,
get bait, beer, some groceries,

but if you want to eat good,
you'll have to catch it,
troll with a nite crawler,

and use a worm threader,
she says, flinging open her register—
even her bills are damp—

this woman from Boston,
forty years back.

No gasoline, no videos,
no newspapers either.
A traveling man
fans himself with his hat.

The news is snow, in meters,
more snow, then freeze,
then melt, and now the runoff,

and if we're lucky, wild orchids
where it's boggy.
The man wanting bug spray

complaining about bugs,
asking where the bugs come from,
when the bugs will die.

Best smelling time for orchids
is way past dark, she says.
Mainly, there's looking
at kinds of water—
running, shining, falling,
then trickling, gathering,

freezing, sloughing, oozing,
melting, the misting,
and the roiling.
What'd I leave out?

Her good-bye is a flick
of a freckled wrist,

which means, *Cast well beyond*
so as not
to spook your dinner.

Ode to a Jeffrey Pine

You tangled and softened the scorch
of sunlight and knew the secret
underground springs. Your greenness
lifted the cool flavor of water, suggesting
a generosity we vowed to learn
but failed and vowed again.
Mad, frantic squirrels
circled your girth, and blue jays
blossomed on your crown.

Every July we practically prayed
to you. But last year you turned
a disastrous lurid orange.

The red-crowned woodpecker drilled you
with a spongy, sick sound. Your cones,
big as coffee cans, splintered
on the ground. Needles fell in clouds,
like shedding hair.

At Kay's store Jack and Larry talk
of casting for rainbows, of sinkers and flashers,
shallows and deeps, saying, *Yeah,
we took that sucker down, no sweat.*
Your stump's wide enough to nap on,
with hack marks from wedges
and ragged gouge bites from the ax.
The work did not go smoothly. The saws
dulled, the men tired. You were so dried out,
you could have gone straight from tree
to dust but resisted.

There are boot-stomped beer cans,
mounds of crushed-out cigarettes,
ripped open Band-Aid wrappers.
You made them work, left nothing
to build with or burn.

Mountain Lake, September

An old chair by the lake keeps rocking,
maybe a ghost has come back for the view.

Sadness fans out, the where have we been
all this time, as piece by piece,
we're nibbled back by the greedy air.

On the sand six people wrestle on masks
and wet suits, their rented second skins.

I'd like to rent a second skin,
one to put on and peel off at will.

All day the El Dorado forest on fire,
and the smoke, sucked over the mountains,
circles South Lake, probably late

for a rendezvous with a blackjack queen
up in Reno. I can't see through the smoke.

Can't think through the wet-suiters' laughter,
wish they'd shut up.
Which they do. Gone into the cold water,

they leave behind a palpable vacuum,
the world much bigger than we thought.

In the water six dark heads bob in a circle,
and that renegade smoke sneaks over the ridge,
heads home to the burning, home to the source.

A DOOR IN THE WALL, AN OPEN FIELD

II

Hell to Heaven Any Given Day

When they wheel you in for surgery, you catch that tone
of voice as they knock you out and make you so alone.

One day we stood at the graves, stooping with flowers,
the sun warmed us, the birds were singing, we were alone.

At that dinner, everyone laughing, good food, good talk,
the swirl of it, let's please go home now, Oh, to be alone.

Bike wreck across the street, everyone trying to help,
call the cops, do first aid, yell out again, all of us quite alone.

Wandering around her house—she's really gone—handling
her things, worrying, wondering where she is now, alone.

There's a splendid sun going down, then clouds ablaze,
call everyone out to see this beauty, together, alone.

You're at your desk paying bills, listening to opera,
and waving your left hand, in time, deliciously alone.

Reading through old letters from when they were alive
I hear their voices, but no, it's me in this room, alone.

Shots, sirens, cops with guns, the please don't move
and that scared old woman shuffles from her house, alone.

What the hell, you never know what the day will bring,
but you live on through it and fall to sleep, again alone.

Hummingbird

He hovered at eye level,
close enough for me to see the green-gold
scoop of his breast and hear his wings
thrum the air. A serene frenzy.
What did those eyes see?

Later my friend said, *You're
dressed in green, like a giant leaf
to him*, but I thought she said,
beef, which explained everything:
I was thick and meaty. He was fine,
a torn-away spirit come to examine
what he'd fled.

Wish I could say I met the bird
face-to-face, knowing he brought
the fierce, short-lived world in close.

But he had that beak. He could lance
an eye, pierce an eardrum—
through to what? I tried running
backward, but ivy tangled my foot,
holding me prisoner, while he
hung upright and watched me flailing.
Nature apparently hated me.

I was all tinny shrillness, while he
beat the evening air into a low hum,
the noise of creation drawing back
before it makes something new.

When I stepped forward he was gone,
the empty place flowing toward the hills,
thousands of bugs taking flight.

Sunday Morning Go to Town

The caged monkey in the corner
of the hotel lobby smells bad,
and he's throwing tangerine slices
through the bars, while Father
consults his bookie. Radio baseball—
it's cheer for the Pirates, while Sinatra
has a world, maybe this one, *on a string*.
All over town the church bells ring, *and not,
little darling, for you and me*. Someone
vacuums the back room, and whoever's
back there can't get it clean enough,
can't call it quits. Whether bluebirds
fly over the white cliffs of Dover
is the day's mystery, also the swinging door
and someone asking, *How'd you get
those nice braids? Can I touch them?*
No, I say. *Go on*, he says, *and let
the nice lady touch your damned braids.*
Funny papers shut pieces of the story
into little rooms and make no sense.
A man arrives, sounding loud and definite,
blasting a clear hole through the day,
telling us that the Brandywine River
has flooded its banks, lost control,
gone into its glory, gone on a bender,
and that he's seen, aside from trees
and doors afloat, he's seen *skunks
and water moccasins hurled together.
Skunks and mocs* on the ride downstream.

Flower Moon

In this full moon they call
Rose Moon, Flower Moon she gets up
and walks barefoot across the sharp-
edged gravel. Her peonies had stayed
clenched in shiny fists for weeks. Like the fists
of the sullen children she'd stood above—
mute and overpowered. Tonight, after
being fed, watered, cursed, pleaded with,
and threatened, they've let themselves go
into layer upon layer of blowsy pink,
arpeggio run of notes transfiguring
the air. She wants to go back inside
and wake him. *Come out here. Come see
what happens despite us.*

Sprouting Moon

He wears the madras jacket,
40 years old, the blue silk
handkerchief saved from Paris.
They drive west to purchase a pitchfork
carved from ash, lathed smooth as cream,
with piercing prongs—the only kind
he'll buy—driving out to where there are
no more telephone poles, no more wires
to string the living into an uneasy quilt.
He stops the car to watch a bearded farmer
plow with his five flaxen-maned horses.
He could offer the man a smoke, unwrap him
a chocolate, but knows he'd politely
decline. Last night's full Sprouting Moon,
pouring cold light, made him imagine
hearing the steel shoes of runaway horses
ringing the asphalt. He squeezes a handful
of dirt and tells her, *Dirt like this,*
here, feel it, he says, *you could grow
anything you ever wanted to grow.*

New Moon

Tonight the old man's dog—
still dying—pants and moans
and leans against his leg. He dreamed
he only dreamed his dog was dying.
Hauls him up from the kitchen floor,
whispers with plaintive rage, *Rusty,
come here, Rusty*, and drags him
out to pee. He points out the planets,
reminding the dog of how Venus, *that one,
look up, dammit*, shines tonight
at its most brilliant and ascends the highest
it'll be for the rest of this century—
the long century closing shut
like the doughnut shop in town;
he and Rusty have to know these things
and hang on to the memory of knowing
the years they roamed the dense woods
and how tenderly the dog once brought him
a speckled thrush egg.

Shame

This is about how our father dealt
with a chicken-killing dog. No way could she hide
from him. He saw red feathers dangling
from her black lips and found the plump body
stashed behind the woodpile. He whistled,
Some enchanted evening, you will meet a stranger,
while uncoiling the twine, and with infinite gentleness,
he tied the limp hen around the dog's neck
and stared until the dog lowered her eyes.
Then he actually invited the kids, the other dogs,
grown people, and even the cats to join him
in staring. Not one of us, praise be, was that
stupid or that complicit. *Bad dog,* he said,
you made me do this. The dog, not escaping
the yellow dangling feet, the smell, the crush
of feathers, the bloody beak, the dog whined
and groveled. Night took too long to arrive
and with it came disrupted sleep. In the morning
no one told about hearing a brush of wings
on the windowpane or seeing the half-moon
spill itself out across the fields and the pond.
All that cold, clean light the moon can't take back.

Ephemeris in South Florida in Winter

Here the old living ones appear to be
in quarantine. They feed off visitors,
clamor to drink whatever we spill.
So they can tell the one story,
which is what any of us are anyhow,
and we listen because

for him it's lunch at one, dinner
at six, evening news with cigar smoke
billowing down the wallpaper,

him telling us daily how winning
is to the swift and charmed,
death's unfair, his life's a curse,
and the out-of-doors is a bother.

Outside the pelican flies, a white cross,
one wing dipped in heaven's ink,
one wing gestures toward the sparkling mall.

Since its cleanliness eases his nerves,
we'll take him tomorrow and the day after
if he wishes, and it seems so little.
Full moon into full eclipse,

slow robing into dark orange, a slow tease.
He's inside, watching it on TV,

saying it's nothing but a matter of vectors
and sight lines, atmospheric debris lit up,
and pretty well explained by science.

He's got this for sleep, that for waking,

takes the rest because, well, otherwise,
in glimmers little hatreds keep stacking,
mean-eyed and shiny-teethed.
Light goes soft over him waving,
his, *Please come back.* A raspy wind
plays through the grapefruit tree.

There's remembering to eat
from the pyramid of food groups,
check the heart rate against the wall chart,
and wear cotton next to the skin.

Oh look, a Golden Orb Spider's got three flies
and veiled the air between this tree and that one.

Snowbound

Once, when I was eight, our mother went on foot
for a doctor through five miles of unplowed snow.

My brother remembers nothing—not waking,
knotted with belly pain, not me and the housekeeper
bundling him into the parlor, hauling logs
to the fire, and ratcheting soup cans open.

Our mother grew small along the fence line,
and then a blur folded into the white landscape.
You could see her footprints,
and then it was silent outdoors.

While, inside, my brother babbled in a made-up
or forgotten or an untranslatable language.
The fir trees cast blue shadows.

By night the snowplow cut a road and brought her home,
brought, too, the doctor. Recovered on his own,
my brother held soldiers while chanting songs
of attack and retreat and he staged

a great funeral, after which he promoted a boy
to general, general to king, king to legend.
But imagine knowing, I tell him, *that she went
and walked a path through the fresh-fallen snow,
just for you. All your life you will remember this.*

Single Thread

When I was a weaver, I chose red silk
to take me to the heart of my creation
and then out, across the loom, back
to whatever life I called mine.

But of course, upon discovering
my little red pathway, buried
between warp and woof, you
thought you'd found a flaw.

But let me remind you
about the weaver who has no exit. After years
breathing wool dust, reeking of lanolin,
and staring into coils of green yarn
and blue, she goes dumb.

You've heard a thousand times
about the trapped fox, whining and snuffling
for hours before she bit through
her paw, through the bone of it,
and ran off into the night.

The mind wants this: a door
in the wall, an open field,
    a narrow path through the woods,
        an open field.

The House of Childhood Talks Back

Your stupid yearly drive-by to stare at me
is delusional. I don't miss you. Or your kin.
Good people have moved in, repainted me,
carpeted me, wall to wall, and stuffed me full

of laughter. Five children who washed
before meals, said grace, and didn't sulk.
The clean-shaven man didn't skip a day
of work. His woman whistled as she scrubbed

my stairs and stuck a succulent ham
in the oven. A huge relief after you people.
Even the dogs smile now. Summer is thick
with roses. Not a spider nor a bat in sight.

Blue-white snowdrifts and snapping fires
light up my winter. No cats pee in the sink.
No one hollers or smacks, no one slams my doors
or guns off in a Buick at midnight.

Gone into the world—oh, those kids—
all so attractive and successful—
their own kids as well, and not—
as I gather from the two old humans here—

not like you people, for whom I did my best
to house your puny dreams. So ravel up
your nostalgia and fling it aside. Take Mercury—
he's ablaze on the horizon. Go stare at him.

Harrow

You can hear the farmer with his tractor
humming above the drying winds of March,
the *Harrow* turning the barren ground.
Then there's that famous *Harrowing of Hell*,

often painted as one hand reaching down
from a fleecy cloud-bank to yank a few souls
up to grace land. The newly saved ones blink
in the glare, little ghosts inquiring
what their redeemer means for them
to do now. And during the Mystery Plays,

the Baker's Guild portrayed the *Harrowing* best:
masters of fire, smoke, and noxious smells,
they amplified the show with clashing pots
and pans, yearly creating a Hell-on-schedule,
Hell-on-earth, Hell-for-an-evening.
Halloo, howls the spotted *Harrier* hound,

having treed the squirrel, howling as if
he'd found a long-lost piece of himself.
Which he'll *Harass*, nearly to death, so then,
we get to the verb, to *Harry*: to afflict, what stops
your breath, strikes you dumb, cools your blood,
as in *Hark*, who goes there?

We'll stop with Chardin's dead *Hare*, stretched out
beside the twined snare that snapped his neck.
You could almost stroke his fur. His breath gone,
his body warm. Easy to imagine there's still time
for him to escape from *Harm*, leap from the canvas
and flee to his burrow.

The Everyday Dog

The speckled dog of exploration whines
until I unlatch the door. The blue dog
of memory howls through the ice fringe.
Always on guard, the mongrel of fury
snaps his teeth at the suckling pups,
even as they lie in their milky sleep.
The world contains far too many dogs.
Even those white clouds are a pack
of lonesome hounds, loping across the sky,
in pursuit of the gray bitch of disdain
whose shadow falls at my feet. Yellow dogs
of mercy run until they drop. Rise up
and run again. One dog, the worthless dog
of the everyday, waits on the threshold
and wags his tail for a treat. At night
I hear him snuffling down the hallway.
He knows I won't ever remember to say,
Good Dog or *Here, Boy*. Unvanquished,
he drinks in every molecule in the room.
Continuously charging the air
with sorrow, he is infinitely patient.

Dowser's Apprentice

The old man hired to find the springs
ambled and peered and whistled.
He handed me the fork of witch hazel
gathered from the riverbank.
It was April. New grass shivering
at our feet, the meadow rolled out
green to the horizon, everything seeming
so ordinary. At first, I resisted the pull
into curvature. *Amplitude is in the hands,*
he said. *Be boneless, give way to what's
under your feet. The Milky Way above us—
that's our shadow river,* he said, and
really, we're all visitors here, briefly
detained in human form. He asked
my parents for permission to rent me
for day wages, to be his hired child wonder,
his water seeker, promising them *we'd find
every hidden spring in the county*. For some
reason they declined, but I was ten and
magnetized for life, my filings aligned,
my purpose unnamed. I am certain that he
still rumbles under the sidewalk: *Don't forget
where you're from—the bitter flavor of watercress,
river silt, and hazel bark*. Some nights,
far from home, I look up to thank him,
star drift or meteor dust—wherever he's gone to.

APPLE BLOSSOMS UNLOOSENED

III

Strategies in Pink

They all tell you red is the color
of rage, of primordial anger, but
they're wrong. The purest,
cleanest flame of razor-brilliant,
quick-slicing rage, it is scentless,
has no image, no sound, nor echo,
it's pink, sometimes a freezing tone,
sometimes burning, no matter;
there it lives, a small, indefatigable
place in your brain. You've been there,
you know it well.

*

You leaned into those lovely pink scrunched bells
because they demanded attention,
dared you to imagine an evocative, spicy scent,
to name it with precision. You let yourself go,
sucked in— sucker—not to paradise—
but through untold realms of odor—an unclean house,
illness, dying, filthy clothing, rancid smoke, wet dog,
rotten food left in the fridge for seven years,
the sour breath of a red-eyed drunk
unforgotten, leaning in for the kiss.

*

An old man with two gold teeth digs
through his mountain of shells to find
the biggest, rosiest conch,
the outside rough as bark, the inside
luminous, smooth as porcelain.
Draws his fingers along the flange—
asking, *lady, all you want is an empty shell?*
Eases his hand deep into the pink spirals
toward the salty, sour home of its animal,
which he ate this morning for breakfast.
Pounded its toughness, soaked it in goat milk,
rolled it in corn flakes, fried in palm oil—
*Should have been here, sweet and juicy,
mm-mm-mmm*, he says.

*

Cancerlandia is not a pink regime.
The anthem is not sung in pink.
There are no pink ribbons, balloons,
T-shirts, roses, thoughts, or songs
in the land of cancerlandia.
In fact there are no festivities,
but if there are, you're not invited.
Roll up your parades and floats,
silence your cheerleaders, take your pink,
every drop of it, and go away.

*

All verb now:

Make holes with a pointed instrument

Pierce with a sword
Hit with a missile
Wound with the weapons of irony,
criticism or ridicule
Cut or perforate
Make a tingling or pinging noise

*

OOOh, aphids on the pink rose. A seething green
colony of them. Ferocious tiny bodies, vibrant
with passion, passionately sucking.
I pinch them off, an entire village, a county,
a slimy, chartreuse, liquid handful. How easily they yield
their bodies to fingers. The black ants, efficient masters
who farmed, milked, shepherded their aphid kine
from one meaty rose to the next, will they miss
their little cattle? Oh, no, they'll raise another herd.

*

First, he wanted the tutu, the tights,
and satin slippers, insisted on nail polish
and lipstick, preferred strawberry sherbet,
small carnations, demanded the tiara, the sparkles,
begged for the light flush of rouge, later it was
tunes in A minor, steak medium rare, scent
of Easter lilies, a glass of rosé, flamingos
on the lawn, several ceramic piglets, all things
pink, and he wouldn't take no for an answer.

*

So yes, I brought home the dress—quivering
in its tissue paper—I was exuberant, and fumbled
the buttons, snagged my zipper. Face-to-face now
in the mirror, it was *Oh*, again *Oh*, I'm head to foot
in the hot pink of an overripe watermelon,
my raucous dress spidered with tiny black roses,
and *oh Lord*, the ruffled pockets, frothy sash,
what was I thinking, a neckline plunging
straight to my old, bony, freckled chest.

*

Don't let anyone fool you. The palest pink?
Considering delicate petals, hidden body
crevices, intricate lace, feathers, cashmere,
seashells, swirled icing on the cake,
no, the most fragile pink is the color
that fills the mind, that breath
of relief after a bout of terror seizes,
tightens its grip, stifles breath,
and then lets go. Take my word.

*

After sunset over the Pacific Ocean, a huge sea
of radiant pink cloud that spills over the horizon
is a languid odalisque of rounded arms, torso,
belly, thighs, and she is uncurling her body
with lazy pleasure,

pillowed between day
and darkness, endlessly reconfiguring her pose

above the sturdy, all-forgiving ocean,
twisting sheets, and dropping hairpins,
hoping for someone, anyone,
to notice

before she's restored,
diminished, to ordinary cloud mass, going,
going gray, going night.

Still Life with Sand in a Picture Locket

The man in shorts drinking beer sends his son,
goggled and flippered, into the Gulfstream.

Sun-spangled and chiseled surface, his beer bottle
is upended, its sullen yellow glass
begrudging the light. The man whistles his boy home.

If you press on memory, where does it spring open,
where does it crumble,
what's the difference when the stranger who serves you
coffee fifty years later has nails that are painted blue?

And a voice that sifts through ash and sand,
the rough sound of low tide,
early morning breeze, old goats among the palms,

Preacher Jack and his horn at dawn, conch fisherman
and the mail boat, the choir up the road getting it right,
choiring the Lord into Sunday. Coconuts dropping.

Sun-bleached shells, the pink cast out,
cast-out line coming up empty,

the way of the line being hard,
weight of the line, baited and tensile,
light and soft in the hand.

Vermeer's Jacket

Wouldn't you love to crawl inside
that luscious gold? To wrap yourself inside
the satiny, charmeuse, rustling raiment,
decked out with an ermine muff,

embellished with tiny teeth and shiny claws.
Call that woman on the canvas
Vermeer's excuse for a yellow immersion,
a tawny daydream edged in fur.

No matter how he arranges her—with the lute,
the maid, the guitar, the letter, the decent pearls—
she's nothing but context
and costume, a recessive coolness

to set off what burns and glows—from brassy sheen
to coppery fire, a yellow to burnish winter's pallor,
to ransom a drop of light—from metallic
to velvety—a concentration of sunlight

dragged back through leaded glass.
Or maybe he brought home
this sumptuous lure to heat up the muse
herself, waiting until the entire household slept

and then, when he burrowed his entire body
into all that silken topaz treasure,
he could paint anything he wanted.

Esthetician to the Elite

One swish and you've got a blush that lasts all day.
What I'm after—*knife-blade cheekbones*—or don't bother.

To create the eternal amusement
Of the impeccably arched brow
You must wax and cut and tweeze

With a vengeance. How do I look—fabulous—*change your
Shadow, change your identity.* It's that simple.

On you the blue-black mascara is *obvious*, suggesting
The elegance of a tiny truth.

Not looking fresh is inexcusable.

I mean when she spilled her tote and out poured, yes, dental
Floss, shower cap, paper clips, yes, and the blue sock,
Old green bra, three candy wrappers, and yes, eight pens.

Concealer is the essence, say no more.

The canvas must be prepared, it must be lavished, it must
Be framed, and my dear, *it has to be seen, seen, seen.*

So I told her, lucky for all that hair. Your one abundance.

When applying bronzing gel, always face
The northern light because

American mirrors contain silica, which greens the skin
And dictates *a whole slew of conclusions.*

Who the hell knows if we have a soul or not,
But the packaging—that's what God gave you to play with.

She looked as if she'd been to a war or a fire or a dustbowl
Or a quagmire and *just didn't take the time.*

Are you terrified yet. I'm dreaming the perfect face.

You never want to look—*here I come in my lipstick!*—as if
The mouth had a life of its own. Which I suppose it does.

I tell them to replenish for everyday degradations. A woman
May exist in the world, but she can't look
Touched by it. Know what I mean?

You must wash off every speck
At bedtime or *go straight to hell.*

Fifty-Minute Hours

Please don't bring the ferrets
again next week, but trouble the water
and drink from the well. Last week everyone
loathed their second born.

Three hundred milligrams
with a martini? There's always Delphi
or black cohosh with ground seahorse
if you boil it two days but beware

of wolfsbane. My Wednesday person
dislikes this dress, says I look like
wallpaper. Let me open the window
and shoo those naughty words

right on out. It was Nina Simone, darlin',
I was there. Your hair looks fabulous,
tell her I said so. Your doctor's
a quack. Go drink from the deeper well.

Some minutes require infinite revision.
You dreamt "cherish" or "perish"?
To get over him, let's find a word
you can sharpen your teeth on.

Lord, if you won't make me brilliant,
trouble the water and forbid me
to whine. One year many sentences
ended in "not." Another year

everyone stepped up to the plate.
Our plate was full, dance card too.
Of course I'll miss you.
Don't explain; don't wear orange.

Summer Nights

Once, in 1978, in Guayaquil, on a jasmine
and tobacco-scented Saturday night in late July,
we strolled along the street

with everyone else, the tinny music streaming
from café doors. We said whatever we thought,

something silly and ordinary, such as *if only nights
like tonight should always happen,* in slow motion
we carried on as if in a suspended droplet
of time, *blablabla*. Perhaps it was because we,

who were young then, had dared to say these words
aloud, that the strange man spun out in circles,
screaming from the bar. He was covered

in blood, his face, his white shirt, his bare arms too. He
wheeled and put his bloody hands on me, lightly
shoving me against the wall, and after he glared at me
with an impersonal, ferocious gaze, he howled

and ran before my friend or I could react. And as
we watched him grab a man down the street, then a small
old woman at the corner, before vanishing, I saw
that everything had occurred in an instant; it seemed

precisely orchestrated. I thought, back then, it meant
something—a corrective, to be blood-
streaked, chastened—as the man leaked his way

into the night. So many people aghast. It seemed that he
created us, recreated us as he tampered

with the inaccessible, deranged core in each person, leaving us uninjured, but more shriveled and stained than we hoped to be. But even this, in years to come, began to seem like such a tiny event.

Walking on the Dead at Montségur

The ruined castle floats above us. It doesn't breathe a hint,
gives nothing away. Once, it sheltered
two hundred unrepentant Cathars until they climbed down
in the bone-numbing cold of February. The castle
and the surrounding fields are quiet. Ever helpful,
the tourist guide quotes the grand inquisitor.
Burn them all, he had insisted, while the Cathars marched
to the funeral pyre, *and God will claim his own.*

The village man makes espresso, saying
he hears crying at night, that his grandfather
did too, that his own mother swears she smells
smoke whenever the church bells ring.

We're curious pilgrims, climbing this mountain,
this overturned grail of rock, through the heat,
slapping flies from our necks and cursing
the slick, white soapstone. We wonder about the history
we brush against, about two hundred persons walking—
so we've been told—joyfully into the annihilating fire.
And now you and I most likely trample some fragment
of a wisp of ash left of people burned
for no good reason on a beautiful mountain.

And seven hundred years later, we're still unsure
what's true about any Heaven, that our souls,

sprung free from flesh, actually rejoin a brilliant
and original clarity, supposedly more pleasing
than life in a trudging, thirsting body. It's hard to know.

Along our path the scrabbly boxwood unleashes
its musty scent. Emerging into sunlight, we finger
the stone walls of this castle, this empty shell,
which seems way too small to have housed so many.

A goshawk whirls, his plummet failing
to strike a small bird's rib cage. Each creature

rearranges itself midflight, as if the encounter
never happened. The birds vanish, the sky
swallowing them back. Far below us
the undulant, green Pyrenees unfold toward Spain.

Streets of Philadelphia

We watched white wine spill,
        sorry it wasn't red,
              which would have been at least a libation
    if not a clear injury. Instead,
we had a cold leakage between us—
        a reluctant pool spreading toward me, toward you—
swallowed by thirsty, white obliging linen.
      When did we become unrecognizable,
like that blue wildflower, five-petaled? I once could
          name it, gather seeds, keep the lineage alive.
    We had one act of grace, watching
the gorgeous, electrically blue Walt Whitman bridge flinging
its body shamelessly across the oblivious river.
        There was slow circling of this city
    and a careful swooping from above.
It's the unsaid words that return
          to haunt us—orphaned, voluble, still hovering.
Your eyes change from brown to darker, absorb the sky, close
the border to a desirable country I won't revisit.
Excuse me while I slip out of another skin,
          each one thinner than the last.

Mushrooms

At noon the bay mare, nodding away flies,
grazes her way across the field to the shade,
her gray foal—in half-shed baby fur—
follows, bored, butting his head against
her flank. From the mushroom houses
a dozen men emerge, blinking into sunlight.
They open their aluminum lunch pails
and unwrap meat sandwiches from wax paper
and snap the Coke lids. They leave behind
the shelves of dark soil gathered
from the county's animals: horses, cattle,
the placid as well as the doomed, the loved,
the nervous walkers of the fence line, the chewers
and the sighers, those who bicker and fuss
in the heat, those who stare—what are they seeing?—
those who roll in the sweet-scented grass,
those who call into the grasshopper air,
those who lug their bodies home for milking.
In their homes of perpetual night,
mushroom spores shape themselves into curve,
gill, and stem, exactly the texture
summer air would choose if air could borrow
any form on Earth it wanted.

Undone

    We enjoyed the lightness of the air, and there was
                a pool of warm light riding the back
of my hand—somewhere I'm always talking to you—the
                    child's black angus steer was
sent by train to slaughter in Indiana, so she hurled herself
          screaming onto the black-and-white
                linoleum floor—it stank of floor wax and
fresh blood—she knew then she couldn't ever—
              there are many small, hard objects, silver
or ivory, left on a bureau—to tell you, to try to make
    time flow backward like the tide—and each object
        I name, ordinary and precious. Now
they say there are planets older than the universe—
              —creation confuses me. There's so much
I need to be true—everything becomes
too late—it's May and white lilacs are a memory
            of a memory, the apple blossoms
unloosened sent flying—
too late for beauty, too soon
for generosity—I'd dive back
        in again—heedless—eyes closed.

Fields

Who's left to call you home—
            where one green hill folds into another—
the way they called when you were young? The comfort
was distant, like the hum of the tractor
                  or the insistent cicadas.
    You were running through tall grass,
someone calling loud out the back door. It was
not that far to the slow, dark river—
          their voices jumped the hills
      to wrap around you—you ran until
they cut this field of pink-flowered clover.
        His hand cupped his mouth to whistle—you left
behind the smell of fresh hay, which made you shiver
for no good reason. Voices pulled you uphill
          to dinner. These huge dogs galloping beside you—
       of course, they were Achilles' immortal, talking
         horses, straight from the supermarket comic book
of the Iliad. That lilac strip of horizon
promised softness. The hot sun drew forth
the scent of fermentation. The red harvester gathered
      row by row, compressing 30 acres of pasture
          into workable bites, bound it
with shining wire, and spit it out in bales. The voices
     grew frail and receded, especially
when the afternoon breezes picked up. The hay
was sold at auction up county
      to black-coated Amish farmers who sniffed
and chewed the green to test for ripeness. You moved on
and moved some more, swallowing up,
        along with its echo, all that color.

Grateful

Thanks for this day in which no one
was shot or robbed on my street,
but no thanks for the three others shot
downtown last night, thanks for a sunset
that was perfect, thanks for small boys
throwing a ball back and again, the arc
against the sky, thanks for Bruce,
the mailman, whistling up the steps,
no thanks for ravens, taking over,
running the small birds away, ravens,
their golden eyes drawing a bead on you
from the rooftops, but thanks for evening,
gardenia blooming, and sound of the trains.

A DESIRE TO MAKE SOMETHING

IV

The Year My Nouns Left Town

When you ask how I mind my age,
you mean *losing my looks*, but I
had no looks to lose. They lived
in the eye of the beholder,
not the beholden.

It's my nouns I miss. I used to plunge
into sentences like a diver
into deep, green water.

My words have gone dry. I hover
at the edge, staring down. There's dust
and ashes. Punishment for devotion
to language, not body.

But every word has a body, comes with
its own smell, texture, way of walking,
how it wants to be held and clothed.

You get embarrassed for me. I am not
embarrassed, I'm merely lost. I've lost
my nouns—my doers, my done to's—
I've swallowed my things of speech.

You say, *Find words for absence*, but I
can't find them either. Blame this
on my *harmonic imbalance*,
coupled with *deprivation* of my *Estragon*,
but he was a character in a different play.

So I try *my estrangement* or *estuary*,
arriving at *estrepe*—the violence
or violation of aftermath. I stop calling
for objects and the glue binding them
to me, me to you, and float in
the synapses—spacious and nameless—
between.

Return of the Heart

Hello, wayward old fool—
won't ask where you've been.
In your absence the rib cage
becomes a picket fence;
there's a shack with smashed windows,
unhinged doors, and hens
scratching the dust.

You're trouble, you manta ray,
you spice of life, prickly pear,
singing half the words while mangling
all the rest. Run off again.

I'll freeze you, then only label you fit
after ten years of boiling. I'll thrash you
with nettles, and there'll be vinegar
to leach your gall, lemon for your bile.

It's a night of fat, bright planets,
airplanes low in the sky—
you come back, all revved and purring
outside my door, my shiny, red
chrome tip convertible.
Take me with you; ruin me again.

What is Implanted in the Body

The voice said, *I'm putting you to sleep.*
So count down with me: ten, nine—of course,
I'll wake you up—eight, seven, ven, ennn…

Titanium is lustrous and ductile, malleable
when hot, brittle when cold. Titanium is light,
found in dirt and igneous rock.
Is essential for missiles.

Before battling the gods, the titans
rubbed the raw ore, a white amorphous powder,
over their bodies for camouflage.
A lot of good it did them, poor souls.

Jacob's excuse was a tiff with the angel.
He came home broken and blessed: off-kilter,
asunder, and aslant. No titanium for him.

Bone, if it chooses, grows into and marries
the porous metal. *Welcome to the neighborhood,*
the body says to metal, *but behave yourself.*

Instructions: before you dump my ashes
in the creek, south of Route 88, west of Carson Pass,
pull out the implants. I've been told
that titanium doesn't melt.

Amputation

A man down the hall yells all night, the sounds bursting
through the eighth floor, east wing's chill sterility.

Everyone here's had a place cut into,
cut off, cut out. *Cut right above
his knee*, says the nurse, sawing the air with her hand

in the awkward way you'd hack at frozen butter,
and because she chooses to save the rest of us—

we, with our monstrous hunger to know—
she won't tell us why or how or his name.

Hunched over walkers we separately trail our racks
of bags with fluids running in, fluids out, and aim
for his door. He's bathed in yellow light,
his back turned; his thin arm dangles. I didn't know

he'd be this young. When he aches
in the empty place, late at night, he shouts, calling out
for the lost loved thing. He shouts
and nothing seems to comfort.

You're a passel of vultures, hisses the night nurse,
catching another of us on crutches,
cruising by his open door to catch a glimpse.

How much can be taken from the body
and a person still want to be held, still told
that the day is fine? The blue blanket,

which drapes his hip, drops off at a steep angle.
Sometimes he dreams about the gone leg
casually slung over another's leg,
as they fall together into sleep.

Syntactic

I had a desire to make something lyrical—
for example, *it smells like rain tonight*—
my fingers were eager to seize the moment's

cool, sweet throat, to write in *the first person,*
to tell you how *I* see the world, in that pronoun *I*,
that ungarnished blazing lighthouse on the page,
which should be easy—if it were clear tonight,

my almanac says, *we'd see Jupiter's moons*—
but look how my left hand, that vagrant interloper,
skitters across the typing keys, and *if*

is born, reborn on the page. The intended *I*
goes *veiled*—no that's too bridal, try *cowled*—
that's too sinister but no matter, no singularity
appears, nothing personal let alone alpha happens,

only this odd subjunctive *if,* a little sniff,
an empty snifter of a word, barely a word,
which at least in Italian's *congiuntivo*
comes with lip-curling flavor, has real aroma,

but in our tongue, our too plain-spoken, *just
the facts, Madam,* the *if*'s a blind
and flailing leap between x and *why*, between stop
and sleep; it's a teasing dislocation

proposing a maybe later future,
and if this, then that, and if I'm tossed
into the air, will fly *as if.*

Passage

That tree dying invisibly for a year,
How quietly some of the living take their leave.

The Egyptians thinking we'd go on as before with oxen,
Trussed sheep, the women weaving linen, coarse and fine.
The brain thrown out—useless for an afterlife,

The heart—the mind's true home—retained.
Everyone knew if the heart was too light, too heavy—
No passage. How do you live toward such a reckoning?

The tree guys say dead on the surface where it counts,
Vital at the core, where it doesn't. For an elm.

Beware of inviting even a tree to be your muse.

In the folded hands of the dead, a polished mirror,
The soul quite fussy about transport—
Three hundreds yards of cotton for eternity's ensemble.
Imagine such tenderness lavished on the living.

Memory's greedy for what's gone—flung light, green breeze,
And for what's still here—the tree guys carrying on

About kids and war and dogs.
Birds in a tizzy, zooming through the empty space.

The Vagrant Spirit as the Good Humor Man

Can't ever plan for his brittle song, his rattling truck.
Sometimes you know in the moment's foreboding:
Something coming,

Something good, as Tony crooned, before Maria,
before the rumble. Time catches its breath
when orange meets vanilla,

a Creamsicle for your jingle-jangle—the man
drives away for years, descending the great valley

one crop at a time—rice, cotton, grapes, lettuce.
He crosses the Mojave to Barstow, swings past
Mono Lake, turns west.

You swear you hear him, but it's another bell,
tolling late mass, or some kid on a bike,
his bell a'twitter.

Around the corner, sang Tony, and whistling
down the river—the couple next door have another kid,
the guy down the block has died, the elm out back as well.

There's a place for us, no, that comes later
when they haven't a prayer, and their long-awaited

has come and gone, as film crackled,
the soundtrack sputtered. There's two kids on a fire escape,
all shining hope. *Dear Officer Krupke,*

we're still no good, the we're no damned good
sung with the sweet flare
our days were burning toward.

Meanwhile, There's Still a War

Sunday in the city, October light at work
resurfacing the bark of the bottlebrush tree.
Put your house in order, say the saints,

but this held-breath day of no rest
throbs like a frayed nerve.

I like thinking about St. Jerome in his study,
the lion snoozing at his feet, the skull on his desk.
He of the wrinkled brow stares off,

pleading with God to send him words that smoke
and sizzle as he writes them down. My flimsy reverie
breaks when the floorboards creak

and the elm creaks back in sympathy.
Cars outside grinding their gears, their people
curse the speed bumps, laugh, and speed away,

as if they'd pulled a fast one,
but on whom? Often I wonder where people drive off to,

and wonder what Rilke meant when he wrote
that if you haven't a home this autumn,
you're out of luck.

Autumn in Oakland with the leaves still green.
A rustling in the air, the continual silk
of what slips through.

Notes on the Solar Storm

The sun has violent moods
every eleven—human—years or so.
It's nothing to the sun but an excess
of imaginable, extravagant energy,
expelled and traveling millions
of inconceivable miles per, what, hour?
Traveling's another wrong word, it is
spewing towards eternity, irradiating
infinite space, splattering our universe
with exuberant-beyond-measure particles,
but by now in the poem, my friend says,
*no people in your poems, put people
at the heart*, and she's nattering on
about why there aren't enough people,
and so, where was I, the sun showering us
with ferocious particles, primordial leftovers,
handfuls, we scoop them up, they litter our air,
suffuse our dust, they bronze-green our pond scum.
Here's a really good handful, hold onto them.

Ordinary Cosmology

Your body rolls toward another in sleep
with the seductive coercion of gravity
a hot summer night takes you in
falling into time, a dizzy delirium

into the seductive coercion of gravity
exhausted remnants of dead stars
falling into time's dizzy delirium
between archer, water bearer, ram

exhausted remnants of burnt-out stars
dark matter pretending to be empty
between archer, water bearer, ram
but it was never really missing

dark matter pretended to be empty
we loved to name: eyelash or milkweed
nothing was ever really missing
at earth's core the small internal planet

we loved naming: eyelash, milkweed
mysterious glue binding a loose weave
at earth's core a small internal planet
suspension of fractured crystals

mysterious glue binding a loose weave
riven, reassembled, axis off-kilter
the suspension of fractured crystals
too hot for liquid, a small hard river

riven, reassembled with axis off-kilter
open the door, walk out, look up
too hot for liquid, a small hard river
sits at the heart out-spinning our reach

open the door, walk out, look up
a hot summer night takes you in
what sits at the heart out-spins our reach
your body rolling toward another in sleep.

The Year's Missing Second

The world has a tiny, missing second,
and every few years we must locate it.

Ask me to describe it, oh, nothing as slow
as a razor's deft cut, a sharpness of breath,
a flame's quick blue to green, all three

quite humanly grasped, this fugitive second

is something to account for, to arrest, lest
earth in its tumble throw noon to twilight,
toss dawn into sunset, what was I thinking

it's that damned God particle, it's him again,

our missing second, what are we waiting for,
let's trap the little bugger, the devil, runt
of the litter, snagging all our scraps, our love,

whining the time's not right, the time's untuned,
that's him alright, toeing the margins,

hoping we'll miss him, let's bring him to order.

Aftermath

Someone someday will cart these books
to a secondhand shop from where, unwanted,
they'll be sent to charity; some stranger

will finger the *Ex Libris* you penned
in your loopy scrawl; it's a funny notion—
to inherit—for handing along what's known

into the unknown. How to carry you forward,
some core of you, and into what place,
we can't tell.

Our dead, they need reassurance,
we imagine: that those who knew you
enough to drop a tidbit into conversation

but not enough to leave a gray pebble
at your favorite spot, they'll vanish.
Quintessential—that's what we say

about the fifth element, the essence
binding those left behind at the table.
This house where something

of your being goes on sliding
through rooms, even now crossing
the threshold, your shadow along the wall,

and the strangers who learned
of your existence over dinner but nothing
about what you enjoyed, after they

have died, after all of us
are gone—there will be still less
of you, right here, in this air.

Reminders to my Biographer

IIIb
Above all, I hated lists. If you're reading this,
you've stolen it from my left front pocket,
and what were you doing there anyhow?

Cii
A few lovers, ex-lovers, might-have-beens,
will-not-have-beens, should-never-have-beens,
and some of the best your definition won't fit.

vi
That my heart was more than once
a hornets' nest, I regret the inconvenience.

23
I preferred the hours of twilight,
black silk, fine hairs on a wrist,
a bag of salty corn chips.

Footnote
Oh sure, go ahead, write what you will,
and remember, I've a long memory. I'm a hellhound
and will dog you to your grave.

Addendum to Footnote
Although last week I did admit that I forgot
your birthday, your middle name, and what,
if anything, I meant to tell you.

7
Carve this on my tombstone:
another wayfarer.

2A
Despite what I already knew at seven,
the Vatican now concedes: that Hell
is not the burning nor the freezing,
but the unendurable absence.

46
Not Monday's nor Tuesday's child,
neither full of nor fair of,
which would have been
an entirely different blessing.

Photo: Eliot Khuner

Helen Wickes was raised on a horse farm in south-eastern Pennsylvania. She attended Vassar College. She now lives in Oakland, California, and worked for many years as a psychotherapist. She received an MFA from the Bennington Writing Seminars. Her first book of poems, *In Search of Landscape*, was published in 2007 by Sixteen Rivers Press. *Dowser's Apprentice* is her second book of poems. Her third book of poems, *Moon Over Zabriskie*, will be published in 2014 by Glass Lyre Press, and in 2015, Sixteen Rivers Press will publish *The World as You Left It*.

Glass Lyre Press, LLC

"Exceptional works to replenish the spirit"

Poetry collections
Poetry chapbooks
Select short & flash fiction
Occasional anthologies

Glass Lyre Press is a small independent literary press interested in work which is technically accomplished and distinctive in style, as well as fresh in its approach and treatment. Glass Lyre seeks writers of diverse backgrounds who display mastery over the many areas of contemporary literature: writers with a powerful and dynamic aesthetic, and ability to stir the imagination and engage the emotions and intellect of a wide audience of readers.

The Glass Lyre vision is to connect the world through language and art. We hope to expand the scope of poetry and short fiction for the general reader through exceptionally well-written books, which call forth our deepest emotions and thoughts, delight our senses, challenge our minds, and provide clarity, resonance and insight.

www.GlassLyrePress.com